10-03-02

DOGS SET II

Dachshunds

Stuart A. Kallen

ABDO & Daughters

visit us at
www.abdopub.com

Published by Abdo & Daughters, 4940 Viking Drive, Suite 622, Edina, Minnesota 55435.

Printed in the United States.

Cover Photo credits: Peter Arnold, Inc.
Interior Photo credits: Peter Arnold, Inc.

Edited by Bob Italia

Library of Congress Cataloging-in-Publication Data

Kallen, Stuart A., 1955-
    Dachshunds / Stuart A. Kallen.
    p. cm. -- (Dogs Set II)
    Includes index.
    Summary: Describes the physical characteristics and habits of these dogs known for their long bodies and short legs, and the care they require as pets.
    ISBN 1-56239-574-2
    1. Dachshunds--Juvenile literature. [1. Dachshunds. 2. Dogs.]
    1. Title. II. Series: Kallen Stuart A., 1955- Dogs. Set II.
    SF429.D25K25   1998
    636.753'8--dc21
                        97-14829
                        CIP
                        AC

Second printing 2002

Contents

Dogs and Wolves—
Close Cousins

Dogs have been living with humans for more than 12,000 years. Today, millions of dogs live in the world. Over 400 **breeds** exist. And, believe it or not, all dogs are related to the wolf.

Some dogs—like tiny poodles or Great Danes—may look nothing like wolves. But under their skin, every dog shares many feelings and **traits** with wolves.

The dog family is called Canidae, from the Latin word *canis*, meaning "dog." The canid family has 37 **species**. They include foxes, jackals, wild dogs, and wolves.

Opposite page: A dachshund.

Dachshunds

Dachshunds (docks-HOONDS) first came from Germany. They were used to hunt badgers. In fact the name dachshund means "badgers dog" in German (dachs means badgers, hund means dog).

Badgers are mean animals that might weigh up to 40 pounds (18 kg). They run into holes underground. Dachshunds needed to be strong and brave to hunt such animals. They also needed to be small enough to chase them underground.

Today, very few dachshunds are used for hunting. They are popular with people who like smaller dogs. Because of their long bodies and short legs, they are sometimes called wiener dogs. Other names given to the dachshund are frankfurter dog, and German sausage dog!

Dachshunds are often called wiener dogs.

What They're Like

    Dachshunds are hardy and strong. They were first bred to drive wild animals out of their underground burrows. This makes them tough and stubborn pets. Some dachshunds are hard to train. They need strong, firm, and loving owners. Dachshunds are fun to play with. They make good watchdogs and they will bark if a stranger comes to the door.

Opposite page:
Dachshunds are
short and sturdy.

Coat and Color

Dachshunds have three different kinds of **coats**—smooth, wire haired, and long haired. The smooth dachshund has a short, smooth coat that is not too thick. The coat has no odor and does not need much brushing or trimming. Smooth dachshunds are the most popular type.

Wirehaired dachshunds are covered with a tight, short, thick, rough outer coat. They have a beard on their chins, and their eyebrows are bushy. The tail hair is coarse.

The long haired dachshund has sleek, wavy hair. Soft, straight, shiny hair grows under the neck and on the underside of the body. The longest hair grows on the backs of the legs and the ears.

One-color dachshunds have red, tan, or reddish yellow hair. Some have short, black stubby hairs mixed in with their color. Their noses and nails are black.

Two-color dachshunds are black, chocolate, gray, or white. They have reddish yellow markings above the eyes, on the sides of their jaws, on their chests, and on parts of their tail.

Dappled dachshunds have a light brown, grayish, or white hair mixed with patches of brown, reddish yellow, or black.

The eyes of all dachshunds are medium sized, oval, and almond shaped. They are dark reddish brown to blackish brown in color.

A long-haired dachshund.

Size

Dachshunds have long bodies and stand low to the ground. They have short, muscular legs. Dachshunds are bred in two sizes—standard and miniature. Standard size dogs weigh between 16 and 32 pounds (7 and 14 kg). The miniature dachshunds weigh under 11 pounds (5 kg).

The head of the dachshund is long and clean cut. The nose is long and narrow. The teeth and jaw are strong and well-developed. The ears are set high on the head. They are long and rounded. The tail of the dachshund should taper to the tip.

Opposite page:
Dachshunds are long
and low to the ground.

Care

Dachshunds make happy members of any family. They are people-pleasers.

Like all dogs, Dachshunds need the same thing humans need: a warm bed, food, water, exercise, and lots of love.

Smooth dachshunds have short **coats** that need very little brushing. Longhaired dachshunds need brushing once a week. Sometimes the longhaired dog will need a bath and its nails clipped. All dogs need shots every year. These shots stop diseases such as **distemper** and **hepatitis**.

As a member of your household, your dog expects love and attention. Dachshunds enjoy human contact and like to play fetch. They love to run and explore outdoors.

Dachshunds enjoy human contact.

Feeding

Like all dogs, Dachshunds like to eat meat. But they need a well-balanced diet. Most dog foods—dry or canned—will give the dog proper **nutrition**.

When you buy a puppy, find out what it has been eating and continue that same diet. A small puppy needs four or five small meals a day. By six months, it will need only two meals a day. By one year, a single evening feeding will be enough.

Dachshunds must be exercised every day so they do not gain weight. Walking, running, and playing together will keep you and your dog happy and healthy. Give your dog a hard rubber ball to play with.

Like any animal, dachshunds need fresh water. Keep water next to the dog's food bowl and change the water daily.

Dachshund puppies need proper nutrition to grow healthy.

Things They Need

A dog needs a quiet place to sleep. A soft dog bed in a quiet corner is the best place for a Dachshund to sleep. A Dachshund should live indoors. If the dog must live outside, give it a dry, **insulated** dog house.

Dachshunds love to play and explore. A fenced-in yard is the perfect home for a dachshund. If that is not possible, use a chain on a runner.

In most cities and towns, a dog must be leashed when going for a walk. It will also need a license. A dog license has the owner's name, address, and telephone number on it. If the dog runs away, the owner can be called.

Opposite page: Dachshunds like to live indoors.

Puppies

A dachshund can have up to six puppies. The dog is **pregnant** for about nine weeks. When she is ready to give birth, she prefers a dark place away from noises. If your dog is pregnant, give her a strong box lined with an old blanket. She will have her puppies there.

Puppies are tiny and helpless when born. They arrive about a half hour apart. The mother licks them to get rid of the birth sac and to help them start breathing. Their eyes are shut, making them blind for their first nine days. They are also deaf for about ten days.

Dogs are **mammals**. This means they drink milk from their mother. After about four weeks, puppies begin to grow teeth. Separate them from their mother and give the puppies soft dog food.

A dachshund puppy.

Glossary

breed: a grouping of animals with the same traits.

coat: the dog's outer covering of hair.

distemper: a contagious disease of dogs and certain other animals caused by a virus.

hepatitis (hep-uh-TIE-tis): an inflammation of the liver caused by a virus.

insulation (in-suh-LAY-shun): something that stops heat loss.

mammal: a group of animals, including humans, that have hair and feed their young milk.

nutrition (new-TRISH-un): food; nourishment.

pregnant: with one or more babies growing inside the body.

species (SPEE-sees): a kind or type.

trait: a feature of an animal.

veterinarian: a doctor trained to take care of animals.

Internet Sites

Dachshund Delights
http://ourworld.compuserve.com/homepages/stemnock/
Dachshund Delights is now in its sixth year of service to 'hundophiles from all over the world. Our Board of Directors consists of five: Peewee (b&t smooth female), Oliver (silver dapple smooth male), Matti (b&t longhair female), Rhett (b&t longhair male), and last but far from least, Stubby (silver dapple longhair female).They command the two human employees, April and Joyce, supervising them vigilantly.

Dachsies@Stgenesi.org
http://www.snowhill.com/~Dogged/dachsie.html
View great Dachshund photos and listen to music, this is a very interactive site, a lot of fun.

Longhaired Dachshunds in Sweden
http://www.amynos.se/taxar/Dachshunds.html
In Sweden we have all of the three varieties of dachshunds; longhaired, shorthaired, and wirehaired; however, the wirehaired dachshunds are the most common. In total, there are nine different breeds of dachshunds combining the three coats and sizes. Dachshunds are very popular and very often used in hunting because of their superb hunting qualities. Because of their charm and beauty they are also much appreciated as pets.

These sites are subject to change. Go to your favorite search engine and type in Dachshunds for more sites.

Index